50 Seasonal Vegetable Dishes Recipes

By: Kelly Johnson

Table of Contents

- Roasted Root Vegetable Medley
- Spring Asparagus Salad
- Winter Squash and Kale Stew
- Grilled Summer Zucchini
- Autumn Pumpkin Soup
- Roasted Brussels Sprouts with Balsamic Glaze
- Spring Pea and Mint Salad
- Summer Corn on the Cob with Herb Butter
- Sautéed Spinach with Garlic and Lemon
- Fall Carrot and Sweet Potato Mash
- Braised Leeks with Thyme
- Roasted Beetroot and Goat Cheese Salad
- Autumn Roasted Cauliflower and Parsnips
- Grilled Eggplant with Tahini Sauce
- Winter Cabbage and Potato Casserole
- Sautéed Swiss Chard with Onions and Pine Nuts
- Spring Fennel and Orange Salad
- Roasted Acorn Squash with Cinnamon
- Summer Tomato and Cucumber Salad
- Sautéed Mushrooms with Garlic and Herbs
- Roasted Brussels Sprouts and Sweet Potatoes
- Zucchini Noodles with Pesto
- Spicy Roasted Carrots with Cumin
- Fall Apple and Butternut Squash Salad
- Herb-Roasted Fingerling Potatoes
- Grilled Peppers with Garlic and Olive Oil
- Winter Vegetable and Lentil Stew
- Baked Stuffed Bell Peppers
- Roasted Radishes with Thyme
- Cabbage Slaw with Apple Cider Vinegar Dressing
- Roasted Broccoli with Lemon Zest
- Braised Red Cabbage with Apples
- Spring Potato and Herb Salad
- Baked Sweet Potatoes with Cinnamon Butter
- Roasted Carrots with Honey and Thyme

- Garlic Parmesan Roasted Cauliflower
- Grilled Portobello Mushrooms
- Spinach and Artichoke Dip with Seasonal Veggies
- Roasted Garlic and Herb Root Vegetables
- Summer Ratatouille
- Winter Squash and Kale Salad
- Sautéed Green Beans with Almonds
- Creamed Spinach with Nutmeg
- Baked Zucchini Fries
- Cauliflower and Potato Gratin
- Fall Roasted Mushroom and Chestnut Salad
- Spicy Tomato and Eggplant Stew
- Grilled Asparagus with Lemon and Parmesan
- Roasted Pumpkin with Sage and Garlic
- Stuffed Acorn Squash with Quinoa

Roasted Root Vegetable Medley

Ingredients:

- 2 large carrots, peeled and cut into 1-inch pieces
- 2 medium parsnips, peeled and cut into 1-inch pieces
- 1 medium sweet potato, peeled and cut into 1-inch cubes
- 1 medium red onion, cut into wedges
- 2 tablespoons olive oil
- 1 teaspoon dried thyme
- 1 teaspoon dried rosemary
- 1/2 teaspoon garlic powder
- Salt and pepper to taste
- **Optional: 1 tablespoon fresh parsley, chopped** (for garnish)

Instructions:

1. Preheat the Oven:
   Preheat your oven to 400°F (200°C).
2. Prepare the Vegetables:
   Peel and chop the carrots, parsnips, sweet potato, and red onion into uniform 1-inch pieces. This ensures even roasting.
3. Toss the Vegetables:
   In a large bowl, combine the chopped vegetables. Drizzle with olive oil, then sprinkle with thyme, rosemary, garlic powder, salt, and pepper. Toss well to coat everything evenly.
4. Roast the Vegetables:
   Spread the vegetables out in a single layer on a baking sheet. Make sure there's enough space between the pieces to allow them to roast properly and become crispy.
5. Bake:
   Roast in the preheated oven for 30-40 minutes, or until the vegetables are tender and lightly browned, tossing halfway through for even roasting.
6. Serve:
   Once roasted, remove from the oven and transfer to a serving dish. Garnish with fresh parsley if desired.

Spring Asparagus Salad

Ingredients:

- 1 bunch fresh asparagus, trimmed and cut into 2-inch pieces
- 1 cup cherry tomatoes, halved
- 1/4 cup red onion, thinly sliced
- 1/4 cup feta cheese, crumbled
- 1/4 cup toasted almonds (or pine nuts)
- 2 tablespoons olive oil
- 1 tablespoon lemon juice
- 1 teaspoon Dijon mustard
- Salt and pepper to taste
- Optional: Fresh herbs like basil or parsley for garnish

Instructions:

1. Blanch the Asparagus:
   Bring a pot of salted water to a boil. Add the asparagus pieces and cook for about 2-3 minutes, until bright green and tender-crisp. Drain and immediately transfer the asparagus to a bowl of ice water to stop the cooking process. Once cooled, drain again and pat dry.
2. Prepare the Dressing:
   In a small bowl, whisk together the olive oil, lemon juice, Dijon mustard, salt, and pepper until well combined.
3. Assemble the Salad:
   In a large bowl, combine the blanched asparagus, halved cherry tomatoes, red onion slices, and crumbled feta cheese.
4. Add the Dressing:
   Drizzle the dressing over the salad and toss gently to coat everything evenly.
5. Garnish and Serve:
   Top with toasted almonds or pine nuts for crunch and sprinkle with fresh herbs if desired. Serve immediately as a light and fresh spring dish!

Winter Squash and Kale Stew

Ingredients:

- 1 medium winter squash (butternut or acorn), **peeled, seeded, and cubed**
- 1 bunch kale, stems removed and chopped
- 1 tablespoon olive oil
- 1 medium onion, diced
- 2 garlic cloves, minced
- 1 carrot, sliced
- 1 celery stalk, diced
- 4 cups vegetable broth
- 1 can (14.5 oz) diced tomatoes
- 1 teaspoon dried thyme
- 1/2 teaspoon ground cumin
- Salt and pepper to taste
- Optional: Crusty bread for serving

Instructions:

1. Sauté the Vegetables:
   In a large pot, heat the olive oil over medium heat. Add the onion, garlic, carrot, and celery. Cook, stirring occasionally, for 5-7 minutes, until the vegetables are softened.
2. Add the Squash and Spices:
   Stir in the cubed winter squash, dried thyme, and cumin. Cook for 2 minutes, allowing the spices to bloom.
3. Simmer the Stew:
   Pour in the vegetable broth and diced tomatoes. Bring the stew to a boil, then reduce the heat to low. Cover and simmer for 20-25 minutes, or until the squash is tender.
4. Add the Kale:
   Stir in the chopped kale and cook for an additional 5-7 minutes, until the kale is wilted and tender.
5. Season and Serve:
   Season with salt and pepper to taste. Serve hot with crusty bread on the side if desired.

Grilled Summer Zucchini

Ingredients:

- 2 medium zucchinis, sliced into 1/4-inch rounds
- 2 tablespoons olive oil
- 1 teaspoon dried oregano
- 1/2 teaspoon garlic powder
- Salt and pepper to taste
- Optional: Fresh lemon juice and chopped fresh herbs for garnish

Instructions:

1. Prepare the Zucchini:
   Preheat your grill or grill pan to medium heat. In a bowl, toss the zucchini slices with olive oil, dried oregano, garlic powder, salt, and pepper.
2. Grill the Zucchini:
   Place the zucchini slices on the grill and cook for 3-4 minutes per side, until grill marks appear and the zucchini is tender but still firm.
3. Garnish and Serve:
   Transfer the grilled zucchini to a serving platter. Optionally, drizzle with fresh lemon juice and sprinkle with chopped herbs for extra flavor. Serve immediately.

Autumn Pumpkin Soup

Ingredients:

- **1 medium pumpkin, peeled, seeded, and chopped** (or 1 can of pureed pumpkin)
- **1 medium onion, diced**
- **2 garlic cloves, minced**
- **2 tablespoons olive oil**
- **4 cups vegetable broth**
- **1 teaspoon ground cinnamon**
- **1/2 teaspoon ground nutmeg**
- **1/4 teaspoon ground ginger**
- **Salt and pepper to taste**
- **1/2 cup coconut milk or cream** (optional for creaminess)
- **Optional: Pumpkin seeds for garnish**

Instructions:

1. Sauté the Onion and Garlic:
   Heat olive oil in a large pot over medium heat. Add the onion and garlic, sautéing until softened and fragrant, about 5 minutes.
2. Cook the Pumpkin:
   Add the chopped pumpkin to the pot and cook for 5-7 minutes. If using fresh pumpkin, you can also roast it before adding for a deeper flavor.
3. Add Broth and Spices:
   Pour in the vegetable broth, cinnamon, nutmeg, and ginger. Bring to a boil, then reduce heat and simmer for 20-25 minutes, or until the pumpkin is soft.
4. Blend the Soup:
   Use an immersion blender to puree the soup until smooth (or transfer in batches to a blender). For a creamier texture, add coconut milk or cream.
5. Season and Serve:
   Season with salt and pepper to taste. Garnish with pumpkin seeds and serve hot.

Roasted Brussels Sprouts with Balsamic Glaze

Ingredients:

- 1 lb Brussels sprouts, trimmed and halved
- 2 tablespoons olive oil
- Salt and pepper to taste
- 2 tablespoons balsamic vinegar
- 1 tablespoon honey
- Optional: Crumbled bacon or toasted almonds for garnish

Instructions:

1. Roast the Brussels Sprouts:
   Preheat your oven to 400°F (200°C). Toss the halved Brussels sprouts with olive oil, salt, and pepper. Spread them in a single layer on a baking sheet.
2. Roast:
   Roast in the preheated oven for 20-25 minutes, tossing halfway through, until crispy and browned.
3. Make the Balsamic Glaze:
   While the sprouts roast, combine balsamic vinegar and honey in a small saucepan over medium heat. Bring to a simmer and cook until thickened, about 5-7 minutes.
4. Toss and Serve:
   Drizzle the balsamic glaze over the roasted Brussels sprouts and toss to coat. Garnish with optional crumbled bacon or toasted almonds. Serve immediately.

Spring Pea and Mint Salad

Ingredients:

- **2 cups fresh peas** (or frozen, thawed)
- **1/4 cup red onion, thinly sliced**
- **1/4 cup fresh mint leaves, chopped**
- **2 tablespoons olive oil**
- **1 tablespoon lemon juice**
- **Salt and pepper to taste**
- **Optional: Crumbled feta cheese or goat cheese for garnish**

Instructions:

1. Blanch the Peas:
   Bring a pot of salted water to a boil. Add the peas and cook for 2-3 minutes, then drain and transfer to a bowl of ice water to stop the cooking process.
2. Assemble the Salad:
   In a large bowl, combine the blanched peas, sliced red onion, and chopped mint.
3. Make the Dressing:
   In a small bowl, whisk together the olive oil, lemon juice, salt, and pepper.
4. Toss and Serve:
   Drizzle the dressing over the salad and toss gently to combine. Garnish with crumbled feta or goat cheese if desired. Serve chilled.

Summer Corn on the Cob with Herb Butter

Ingredients:

- 4 ears of corn, husked
- 1/2 cup unsalted butter, softened
- 2 tablespoons fresh parsley, chopped
- 1 tablespoon fresh basil, chopped
- 1 teaspoon garlic powder
- Salt and pepper to taste

Instructions:

1. Grill the Corn:
   Preheat your grill to medium-high heat. Place the corn directly on the grill and cook, turning occasionally, for about 10-12 minutes, until the kernels are tender and slightly charred.
2. Make the Herb Butter:
   In a small bowl, mix together the softened butter, parsley, basil, garlic powder, salt, and pepper.
3. Serve:
   Once the corn is grilled, remove it from the heat. Spread the herb butter generously over the hot corn. Serve immediately.

Sautéed Spinach with Garlic and Lemon

Ingredients:

- 2 tablespoons olive oil
- 3 garlic cloves, minced
- 10 oz fresh spinach, washed
- Juice of 1/2 lemon
- Salt and pepper to taste
- Optional: Red pepper flakes for a little heat

Instructions:

1. Heat the Oil:
   In a large skillet, heat the olive oil over medium heat. Add the minced garlic and sauté for about 1 minute until fragrant, being careful not to burn the garlic.
2. Cook the Spinach:
   Add the fresh spinach in batches, allowing it to wilt down before adding more. Cook for about 3-4 minutes, stirring occasionally.
3. Finish the Dish:
   Once the spinach is fully wilted, squeeze the lemon juice over the top. Season with salt, pepper, and optional red pepper flakes. Serve immediately.

Fall Carrot and Sweet Potato Mash

Ingredients:

- **4 medium carrots, peeled and chopped**
- **2 medium sweet potatoes, peeled and chopped**
- **1/4 cup unsalted butter**
- **1/4 cup heavy cream** (or milk)
- **Salt and pepper to taste**
- **Optional: Fresh thyme or rosemary for garnish**

Instructions:

1. Cook the Vegetables:
   In a large pot, bring water to a boil and add the carrots and sweet potatoes. Cook until tender, about 15-20 minutes. Drain the vegetables.
2. Mash:
   Return the vegetables to the pot. Add the butter and cream. Mash with a potato masher until smooth and creamy.
3. Season and Serve:
   Season with salt and pepper to taste. Garnish with fresh herbs if desired, and serve warm.

Braised Leeks with Thyme

Ingredients:

- **4 leeks, trimmed and sliced**
- **1 tablespoon olive oil**
- **1 cup vegetable broth**
- **1 teaspoon fresh thyme leaves** (or 1/2 teaspoon dried thyme)
- **Salt and pepper to taste**

Instructions:

1. Sauté the Leeks:
   In a large skillet, heat the olive oil over medium heat. Add the sliced leeks and cook, stirring occasionally, for 5-7 minutes until softened.
2. Add the Broth and Thyme:
   Pour in the vegetable broth and add the thyme. Bring to a simmer, cover, and cook for about 15-20 minutes, until the leeks are tender.
3. Season and Serve:
   Season with salt and pepper. Serve warm.

Roasted Beetroot and Goat Cheese Salad

Ingredients:

- 3 medium beets, peeled and cut into cubes
- 2 tablespoons olive oil
- Salt and pepper to taste
- 4 cups mixed salad greens (arugula, spinach, etc.)
- 1/4 cup goat cheese, crumbled
- 1/4 cup walnuts, toasted
- 1 tablespoon balsamic vinegar
- Optional: Fresh herbs for garnish

Instructions:

1. Roast the Beets:
   Preheat your oven to 400°F (200°C). Toss the beet cubes with olive oil, salt, and pepper. Spread on a baking sheet and roast for 25-30 minutes, until tender.
2. Assemble the Salad:
   In a large bowl, combine the roasted beets with salad greens. Top with crumbled goat cheese and toasted walnuts.
3. Dress the Salad:
   Drizzle with balsamic vinegar and toss gently. Garnish with fresh herbs if desired and serve immediately.

Autumn Roasted Cauliflower and Parsnips

Ingredients:

- 1 small cauliflower, cut into florets
- 3 parsnips, peeled and cut into sticks
- 2 tablespoons olive oil
- 1 teaspoon ground cumin
- Salt and pepper to taste
- Optional: Fresh parsley for garnish

Instructions:

1. Preheat the Oven:
   Preheat your oven to 400°F (200°C). Line a baking sheet with parchment paper.
2. Roast the Vegetables:
   Toss the cauliflower and parsnips with olive oil, cumin, salt, and pepper. Spread them out on the prepared baking sheet.
3. Bake:
   Roast for 25-30 minutes, or until the vegetables are tender and golden, tossing halfway through for even roasting.
4. Serve:
   Garnish with fresh parsley if desired and serve warm.

Grilled Eggplant with Tahini Sauce

Ingredients:

- 2 medium eggplants, sliced into 1/2-inch rounds
- 2 tablespoons olive oil
- Salt and pepper to taste
- 1/4 cup tahini
- 2 tablespoons lemon juice
- 1 tablespoon water (to thin the sauce)
- 1 garlic clove, minced
- Fresh parsley for garnish

Instructions:

1. Grill the Eggplant:
   Preheat the grill to medium-high heat. Brush both sides of the eggplant slices with olive oil and season with salt and pepper. Grill for 3-4 minutes per side, until tender and charred.
2. Make the Tahini Sauce:
   In a small bowl, whisk together tahini, lemon juice, water, and minced garlic until smooth.
3. Serve:
   Arrange the grilled eggplant on a serving platter. Drizzle with tahini sauce and garnish with fresh parsley. Serve immediately.

Winter Cabbage and Potato Casserole

Ingredients:

- 1 small head of cabbage, shredded
- 3 medium potatoes, peeled and thinly sliced
- 1 medium onion, diced
- 2 tablespoons olive oil
- 1 cup vegetable broth
- 1 teaspoon dried thyme
- Salt and pepper to taste
- **1/2 cup grated cheese** (optional)

Instructions:

1. Sauté the Vegetables:
   Preheat the oven to 375°F (190°C). Heat olive oil in a large skillet. Add the onion and sauté for 3-4 minutes until softened. Add the cabbage and cook until slightly wilted, about 5 minutes.
2. Layer the Casserole:
   In a baking dish, layer the sliced potatoes, sautéed cabbage, and onions. Pour in the vegetable broth, sprinkle with thyme, salt, and pepper.
3. Bake:
   Cover the dish with foil and bake for 40-45 minutes, until the potatoes are tender. If using cheese, sprinkle it on top during the last 10 minutes of baking and return to the oven until melted.

Sautéed Swiss Chard with Onions and Pine Nuts

Ingredients:

- 1 bunch Swiss chard, chopped
- 1 medium onion, sliced
- 2 tablespoons olive oil
- 1/4 cup pine nuts, toasted
- Salt and pepper to taste
- 1 tablespoon lemon juice (optional)

Instructions:

1. Sauté the Onion:
   Heat the olive oil in a large skillet over medium heat. Add the onion and cook for 5 minutes, until softened.
2. Cook the Swiss Chard:
   Add the Swiss chard to the skillet and cook for 4-5 minutes, until wilted.
3. Finish the Dish:
   Stir in the toasted pine nuts and season with salt, pepper, and optional lemon juice. Serve warm.

Spring Fennel and Orange Salad

Ingredients:

- 1 fennel bulb, thinly sliced
- 2 oranges, peeled and segmented
- 1 tablespoon olive oil
- 1 tablespoon white wine vinegar
- Salt and pepper to taste
- Optional: Fresh dill or parsley for garnish

Instructions:

1. Prepare the Salad:
   In a large bowl, combine the sliced fennel and orange segments.
2. Make the Dressing:
   In a small bowl, whisk together the olive oil, white wine vinegar, salt, and pepper.
3. Assemble and Serve:
   Drizzle the dressing over the fennel and orange mixture. Garnish with fresh dill or parsley if desired. Serve chilled.

Roasted Acorn Squash with Cinnamon

Ingredients:

- 2 acorn squashes, halved and seeded
- 2 tablespoons olive oil
- 1 teaspoon ground cinnamon
- Salt and pepper to taste
- 1 tablespoon maple syrup (optional)

Instructions:

1. Preheat the Oven:
   Preheat your oven to 400°F (200°C). Line a baking sheet with parchment paper.
2. Prepare the Squash:
   Drizzle the acorn squash halves with olive oil and sprinkle with cinnamon, salt, and pepper. Place the squash halves cut-side down on the baking sheet.
3. Roast the Squash:
   Roast in the preheated oven for 30-35 minutes, until tender when pierced with a fork.
4. Serve:
   If desired, drizzle with maple syrup before serving. Serve warm.

Summer Tomato and Cucumber Salad

Ingredients:

- 3 medium tomatoes, chopped
- 1 cucumber, sliced
- 1/4 cup red onion, thinly sliced
- 2 tablespoons olive oil
- 1 tablespoon red wine vinegar
- Salt and pepper to taste
- Fresh basil for garnish

Instructions:

1. Combine the Vegetables:
   In a large bowl, combine the chopped tomatoes, cucumber slices, and red onion.
2. Dress the Salad:
   Drizzle with olive oil and red wine vinegar. Toss gently to coat.
3. Season and Serve:
   Season with salt and pepper to taste. Garnish with fresh basil leaves. Serve immediately.

Sautéed Mushrooms with Garlic and Herbs

Ingredients:

- 8 oz mushrooms, sliced
- 2 tablespoons olive oil
- 2 garlic cloves, minced
- 1 tablespoon fresh thyme leaves
- Salt and pepper to taste

Instructions:

1. Heat the Oil:
   Heat olive oil in a large skillet over medium heat.
2. Cook the Mushrooms:
   Add the sliced mushrooms to the skillet and cook for 5-7 minutes, until they release their moisture and begin to brown.
3. Add the Garlic and Herbs:
   Stir in the minced garlic and thyme. Continue to cook for another 2-3 minutes, until the garlic is fragrant.
4. Season and Serve:
   Season with salt and pepper to taste. Serve warm.

Roasted Brussels Sprouts and Sweet Potatoes

Ingredients:

- 1 lb Brussels sprouts, trimmed and halved
- 2 medium sweet potatoes, peeled and cubed
- 2 tablespoons olive oil
- 1 teaspoon ground paprika
- Salt and pepper to taste

Instructions:

1. Preheat the Oven:
   Preheat your oven to 400°F (200°C). Line a baking sheet with parchment paper.
2. Prepare the Vegetables:
   Toss the Brussels sprouts and sweet potato cubes with olive oil, paprika, salt, and pepper.
3. Roast the Vegetables:
   Spread the vegetables in a single layer on the baking sheet. Roast for 25-30 minutes, stirring halfway through, until tender and slightly caramelized.
4. Serve:
   Serve warm as a hearty side dish.

Zucchini Noodles with Pesto

Ingredients:

- **4 medium zucchinis, spiralized into noodles**
- **1/2 cup pesto** (store-bought or homemade)
- **1 tablespoon olive oil**
- **Salt and pepper to taste**
- **Optional: Grated Parmesan cheese for garnish**

Instructions:

1. Sauté the Zucchini Noodles:
   Heat olive oil in a large skillet over medium heat. Add the zucchini noodles and cook for 2-3 minutes, until tender but still slightly firm.
2. Add the Pesto:
   Stir in the pesto and toss to coat the noodles evenly. Cook for another 1-2 minutes to heat through.
3. Season and Serve:
   Season with salt and pepper to taste. Garnish with grated Parmesan cheese if desired and serve warm.

Spicy Roasted Carrots with Cumin

Ingredients:

- 6 medium carrots, peeled and cut into sticks
- 2 tablespoons olive oil
- 1 teaspoon ground cumin
- 1/2 teaspoon chili powder
- Salt and pepper to taste

Instructions:

1. Preheat the Oven:
   Preheat your oven to 400°F (200°C). Line a baking sheet with parchment paper.
2. Prepare the Carrots:
   Toss the carrot sticks with olive oil, cumin, chili powder, salt, and pepper.
3. Roast the Carrots:
   Spread the carrots in a single layer on the baking sheet. Roast for 20-25 minutes, until tender and caramelized.
4. Serve:
   Serve immediately as a spicy and flavorful side dish.

Fall Apple and Butternut Squash Salad

Ingredients:

- 2 cups roasted butternut squash cubes
- 2 apples, thinly sliced
- 4 cups mixed greens (arugula, spinach, etc.)
- 1/4 cup dried cranberries
- 1/4 cup walnuts, toasted
- 2 tablespoons olive oil
- 1 tablespoon apple cider vinegar
- 1 teaspoon honey
- Salt and pepper to taste

Instructions:

1. Prepare the Salad:
   In a large bowl, combine the roasted butternut squash cubes, apple slices, mixed greens, dried cranberries, and toasted walnuts.
2. Make the Dressing:
   In a small bowl, whisk together olive oil, apple cider vinegar, honey, salt, and pepper.
3. Toss and Serve:
   Drizzle the dressing over the salad and toss gently to combine. Serve immediately.

Herb-Roasted Fingerling Potatoes

Ingredients:

- **1 lb fingerling potatoes**, halved
- **2 tbsp olive oil**
- **2 tsp dried rosemary**
- **2 tsp dried thyme**
- **2 cloves garlic**, minced
- **Salt and pepper** to taste

Instructions:

1. Preheat the oven to 400°F (200°C). Line a baking sheet with parchment paper.
2. Toss the fingerling potatoes with olive oil, rosemary, thyme, garlic, salt, and pepper.
3. Spread the potatoes evenly on the baking sheet and roast for 25-30 minutes, or until golden and crispy, flipping halfway through.
4. Serve immediately as a savory side dish.

Grilled Peppers with Garlic and Olive Oil

Ingredients:

- **4 bell peppers**, sliced into strips
- **2 tbsp olive oil**
- **2 cloves garlic**, minced
- **1 tsp dried oregano**
- **Salt and pepper** to taste

Instructions:

1. Preheat the grill to medium heat.
2. Toss the pepper strips with olive oil, garlic, oregano, salt, and pepper.
3. Grill the peppers for 5-7 minutes, turning occasionally, until tender and slightly charred.
4. Serve warm as a smoky, flavorful side.

Winter Vegetable and Lentil Stew

Ingredients:

- **1 cup dried lentils**, rinsed
- **2 carrots**, chopped
- **2 parsnips**, chopped
- **1 large potato**, peeled and diced
- **1 onion**, chopped
- **2 cloves garlic**, minced
- **4 cups vegetable broth**
- **2 tsp dried thyme**
- **Salt and pepper** to taste
- **2 tbsp olive oil**

Instructions:

1. In a large pot, heat olive oil over medium heat. Add the onions and garlic, sautéing until softened.
2. Add the carrots, parsnips, potatoes, lentils, vegetable broth, thyme, salt, and pepper. Bring to a boil.
3. Reduce the heat to low, cover, and simmer for 30-40 minutes, or until the lentils and vegetables are tender.
4. Serve warm as a hearty, comforting stew.

Baked Stuffed Bell Peppers

Ingredients:

- **4 bell peppers**, tops cut off and seeds removed
- **1 cup cooked quinoa** or rice
- **1 can black beans**, drained and rinsed
- **1 cup corn kernels**
- **1 tsp cumin**
- **1 tsp chili powder**
- **Salt and pepper** to taste
- **1 cup shredded cheese** (optional)

Instructions:

1. Preheat the oven to 375°F (190°C). Place the bell peppers in a baking dish.
2. In a bowl, mix the quinoa or rice, black beans, corn, cumin, chili powder, salt, and pepper.
3. Stuff the bell peppers with the mixture and top with shredded cheese if desired.
4. Cover the dish with foil and bake for 25-30 minutes, until the peppers are tender.
5. Serve immediately.

Roasted Radishes with Thyme

Ingredients:

- **1 lb radishes**, trimmed and halved
- **2 tbsp olive oil**
- **2 tsp fresh thyme**
- **Salt and pepper** to taste

Instructions:

1. Preheat the oven to 400°F (200°C). Line a baking sheet with parchment paper.
2. Toss the radishes with olive oil, thyme, salt, and pepper.
3. Spread the radishes in a single layer on the baking sheet and roast for 20-25 minutes, until tender and golden.
4. Serve warm as a flavorful side dish.

Cabbage Slaw with Apple Cider Vinegar Dressing

Ingredients:

- **1/2 small head of cabbage**, shredded
- **1 carrot**, grated
- **2 tbsp apple cider vinegar**
- **2 tbsp olive oil**
- **1 tsp Dijon mustard**
- **1 tsp honey**
- **Salt and pepper** to taste

Instructions:

1. In a large bowl, combine the shredded cabbage and grated carrot.
2. In a small bowl, whisk together the apple cider vinegar, olive oil, Dijon mustard, honey, salt, and pepper.
3. Pour the dressing over the cabbage mixture and toss to combine.
4. Chill in the refrigerator for 30 minutes before serving.

Roasted Broccoli with Lemon Zest

Ingredients:

- 1 lb broccoli florets
- 2 tbsp olive oil
- 1 lemon, zested
- **Salt and pepper** to taste

Instructions:

1. Preheat the oven to 400°F (200°C). Line a baking sheet with parchment paper.
2. Toss the broccoli florets with olive oil, lemon zest, salt, and pepper.
3. Spread the broccoli on the baking sheet and roast for 15-20 minutes, or until tender and slightly crispy.
4. Serve warm as a simple, zesty side dish.

Braised Red Cabbage with Apples

Ingredients:

- **1 small head red cabbage**, shredded
- **2 apples**, peeled and sliced
- **1 onion**, sliced
- **2 tbsp olive oil**
- **1/4 cup apple cider vinegar**
- **1/4 cup apple juice**
- **1 tbsp brown sugar**
- **1/2 tsp ground cinnamon**
- **Salt and pepper** to taste

Instructions:

1. In a large pot, heat olive oil over medium heat. Add the onions and sauté until soft.
2. Add the shredded cabbage, apples, apple cider vinegar, apple juice, brown sugar, cinnamon, salt, and pepper.
3. Cover and simmer for 30-40 minutes, stirring occasionally, until the cabbage is tender.
4. Serve warm as a sweet and savory side dish.

Spring Potato and Herb Salad

Ingredients:

- **1 lb baby potatoes**, boiled and halved
- **1/4 cup fresh parsley**, chopped
- **1/4 cup fresh dill**, chopped
- **2 tbsp olive oil**
- **1 tbsp lemon juice**
- **Salt and pepper** to taste

Instructions:

1. Boil the baby potatoes in salted water for about 10-15 minutes until tender. Drain and allow to cool.
2. In a bowl, combine the potatoes, parsley, dill, olive oil, lemon juice, salt, and pepper.
3. Toss gently to combine and serve chilled as a fresh, herbaceous side dish.

Baked Sweet Potatoes with Cinnamon Butter

Ingredients:

- **4 medium sweet potatoes**
- **2 tbsp butter**, softened
- **1 tsp ground cinnamon**
- **1 tbsp maple syrup** (optional)
- **Salt** to taste

Instructions:

1. Preheat the oven to 400°F (200°C). Pierce the sweet potatoes with a fork and place them on a baking sheet.
2. Bake for 45-60 minutes, until tender and easily pierced with a fork.
3. While the potatoes bake, mix the softened butter with cinnamon and maple syrup (if using).
4. Once the potatoes are cooked, slice them open and top with the cinnamon butter.
5. Serve warm as a sweet and comforting side dish.

Roasted Carrots with Honey and Thyme

Ingredients:

- **1 lb carrots**, peeled and cut into sticks
- **2 tbsp olive oil**
- **2 tbsp honey**
- **2 tsp fresh thyme** (or 1 tsp dried thyme)
- **Salt and pepper** to taste

Instructions:

1. Preheat the oven to 400°F (200°C). Line a baking sheet with parchment paper.
2. Toss the carrots with olive oil, honey, thyme, salt, and pepper.
3. Spread them in a single layer on the baking sheet.
4. Roast for 20-25 minutes, turning halfway through, until tender and caramelized.
5. Serve immediately for a sweet and savory side dish.

Garlic Parmesan Roasted Cauliflower

Ingredients:

- **1 head cauliflower**, cut into florets
- **2 tbsp olive oil**
- **3 cloves garlic**, minced
- **1/2 cup grated Parmesan cheese**
- **Salt and pepper** to taste

Instructions:

1. Preheat the oven to 400°F (200°C). Line a baking sheet with parchment paper.
2. Toss the cauliflower florets with olive oil, garlic, salt, and pepper.
3. Spread the florets on the baking sheet and roast for 20-25 minutes, until tender and slightly crispy.
4. Remove from the oven and sprinkle with Parmesan cheese.
5. Serve warm as a cheesy, flavorful side dish.

Grilled Portobello Mushrooms

Ingredients:

- **4 large Portobello mushrooms**, stems removed
- **2 tbsp olive oil**
- **1 tbsp balsamic vinegar**
- **2 cloves garlic**, minced
- **Salt and pepper** to taste

Instructions:

1. Preheat the grill to medium-high heat.
2. In a small bowl, whisk together olive oil, balsamic vinegar, garlic, salt, and pepper.
3. Brush the mushrooms with the olive oil mixture.
4. Grill the mushrooms for 5-7 minutes per side, until tender and grill marks appear.
5. Serve warm as a savory vegetarian option.

Spinach and Artichoke Dip with Seasonal Veggies

Ingredients:

- **1 cup frozen spinach**, thawed and squeezed dry
- **1 cup canned artichoke hearts**, drained and chopped
- **1/2 cup cream cheese**, softened
- **1/4 cup sour cream**
- **1/4 cup grated Parmesan cheese**
- **1/2 cup shredded mozzarella cheese**
- **1 clove garlic**, minced
- **Salt and pepper** to taste
- **Seasonal veggies** for dipping (carrot sticks, cucumber slices, bell pepper strips)

Instructions:

1. Preheat the oven to 375°F (190°C). In a bowl, combine spinach, artichokes, cream cheese, sour cream, Parmesan, mozzarella, garlic, salt, and pepper.
2. Transfer the mixture to a small baking dish and bake for 20-25 minutes, until bubbly and golden on top.
3. Serve warm with a platter of seasonal veggies for dipping.

Roasted Garlic and Herb Root Vegetables

Ingredients:

- **2 large carrots**, peeled and chopped
- **2 parsnips**, peeled and chopped
- **1 sweet potato**, peeled and cubed
- **2 tbsp olive oil**
- **3 cloves garlic**, minced
- **2 tsp fresh rosemary**, chopped
- **2 tsp fresh thyme**, chopped
- **Salt and pepper** to taste

Instructions:

1. Preheat the oven to 400°F (200°C). Line a baking sheet with parchment paper.
2. Toss the root vegetables with olive oil, garlic, rosemary, thyme, salt, and pepper.
3. Spread the vegetables evenly on the baking sheet.
4. Roast for 30-35 minutes, turning halfway through, until tender and caramelized.
5. Serve warm as a comforting side dish.

Summer Ratatouille

Ingredients:

- **2 zucchinis**, sliced
- **1 eggplant**, diced
- **2 tomatoes**, diced
- **1 red bell pepper**, chopped
- **1 yellow bell pepper**, chopped
- **1 onion**, chopped
- **2 cloves garlic**, minced
- **2 tbsp olive oil**
- **1 tsp dried oregano**
- **Salt and pepper** to taste

Instructions:

1. Heat olive oil in a large skillet over medium heat. Add the onion and garlic and sauté until softened.
2. Add the zucchini, eggplant, peppers, and tomatoes. Stir in oregano, salt, and pepper.
3. Cook, stirring occasionally, for 15-20 minutes, until the vegetables are tender and well combined.
4. Serve warm as a savory and colorful summer dish.

Winter Squash and Kale Salad

Ingredients:

- **1 small winter squash** (such as butternut), peeled, seeded, and cubed
- **2 tbsp olive oil**
- **1 tsp ground cinnamon**
- **1/2 tsp ground nutmeg**
- **4 cups kale**, chopped and massaged with olive oil
- **1/4 cup dried cranberries**
- **1/4 cup toasted pumpkin seeds**
- **1 tbsp apple cider vinegar**
- **Salt and pepper** to taste

Instructions:

1. Preheat the oven to 400°F (200°C). Toss the squash cubes with olive oil, cinnamon, nutmeg, salt, and pepper.
2. Roast the squash on a baking sheet for 20-25 minutes, until tender.
3. In a large bowl, toss the massaged kale, roasted squash, cranberries, and pumpkin seeds.
4. Drizzle with apple cider vinegar and toss again. Serve warm or at room temperature.

Sautéed Green Beans with Almonds

Ingredients:

- **1 lb green beans**, trimmed
- **2 tbsp olive oil**
- **2 cloves garlic**, minced
- **1/4 cup sliced almonds**
- **Salt and pepper** to taste

Instructions:

1. In a large skillet, heat olive oil over medium heat. Add the garlic and sauté until fragrant.
2. Add the green beans and cook for 5-7 minutes, stirring occasionally, until tender-crisp.
3. Add the sliced almonds and cook for another 2-3 minutes until the almonds are lightly toasted.
4. Season with salt and pepper and serve warm as a crunchy, flavorful side dish.

Creamed Spinach with Nutmeg

Ingredients:

- **1 lb fresh spinach** (or 2 lbs frozen spinach, thawed and squeezed dry)
- **2 tbsp butter**
- **1 small onion**, finely chopped
- **2 cloves garlic**, minced
- **1/2 cup heavy cream**
- **1/4 tsp ground nutmeg**
- **Salt and pepper** to taste
- **1/2 cup grated Parmesan cheese** (optional)

Instructions:

1. In a large skillet, melt butter over medium heat. Add the onion and garlic, cooking until soft and fragrant (about 3-4 minutes).
2. Add the spinach (if using fresh, cook until wilted; if using frozen, heat through).
3. Stir in the cream and nutmeg, cooking for an additional 2-3 minutes until the mixture thickens slightly.
4. Season with salt and pepper to taste. Optionally, stir in Parmesan cheese until melted and smooth.
5. Serve warm as a rich and flavorful side dish.

Baked Zucchini Fries

Ingredients:

- **2 medium zucchinis**, cut into fries
- **1/2 cup breadcrumbs** (preferably panko)
- **1/4 cup grated Parmesan cheese**
- **1 tsp garlic powder**
- **1 tsp onion powder**
- **Salt and pepper** to taste
- **2 eggs**, beaten
- **Olive oil spray** for baking

Instructions:

1. Preheat the oven to 425°F (220°C). Line a baking sheet with parchment paper and lightly spray with olive oil.
2. In a shallow bowl, combine breadcrumbs, Parmesan, garlic powder, onion powder, salt, and pepper.
3. Dip the zucchini fries into the beaten eggs, then coat with the breadcrumb mixture, pressing gently to adhere.
4. Place the coated fries on the prepared baking sheet.
5. Spray the fries with a light coat of olive oil.
6. Bake for 20-25 minutes, flipping halfway through, until golden and crispy.
7. Serve warm with your favorite dipping sauce.

Cauliflower and Potato Gratin

Ingredients:

- **2 medium potatoes**, peeled and sliced
- **1 small cauliflower**, cut into florets
- **1 cup heavy cream**
- **1/2 cup grated Gruyère cheese** (or cheese of choice)
- **1/2 tsp garlic powder**
- **Salt and pepper** to taste
- **2 tbsp butter**, for greasing the dish

Instructions:

1. Preheat the oven to 375°F (190°C). Grease a baking dish with butter.
2. In a saucepan, heat the heavy cream over low heat, stirring occasionally, until warmed through. Season with garlic powder, salt, and pepper.
3. In the greased baking dish, layer the potato slices, followed by cauliflower florets. Pour the cream mixture over the top.
4. Sprinkle the grated cheese evenly over the top.
5. Cover the dish with foil and bake for 30 minutes. Remove the foil and bake for an additional 20-25 minutes until the potatoes are tender and the top is golden.
6. Serve warm as a comforting and creamy side dish.

Fall Roasted Mushroom and Chestnut Salad

Ingredients:

- **2 cups mixed mushrooms** (such as cremini, shiitake, and oyster), sliced
- **1 cup cooked chestnuts**, chopped
- **2 tbsp olive oil**
- **1 tbsp balsamic vinegar**
- **1 tsp fresh thyme** (or 1/2 tsp dried thyme)
- **4 cups mixed greens** (such as arugula, spinach, and kale)
- **Salt and pepper** to taste
- **1/4 cup crumbled feta cheese** (optional)

Instructions:

1. Preheat the oven to 400°F (200°C). Toss the mushrooms and chestnuts with olive oil, balsamic vinegar, thyme, salt, and pepper.
2. Spread the mixture on a baking sheet and roast for 15-20 minutes, until the mushrooms are tender and golden.
3. While the mushrooms and chestnuts roast, toss the mixed greens with a drizzle of olive oil and vinegar.
4. Once the mushrooms and chestnuts are done, allow them to cool slightly before tossing with the greens.
5. Optionally, top with crumbled feta cheese before serving.

Spicy Tomato and Eggplant Stew

Ingredients:

- **1 medium eggplant**, diced
- **2 tbsp olive oil**
- **1 onion**, chopped
- **2 cloves garlic**, minced
- **1 can (14 oz) diced tomatoes**
- **1 tbsp tomato paste**
- **1 tsp smoked paprika**
- **1/2 tsp chili flakes** (adjust for spice level)
- **1/2 cup vegetable broth**
- **Salt and pepper** to taste

Instructions:

1. In a large pot, heat olive oil over medium heat. Add the onion and garlic, cooking until soft.
2. Add the diced eggplant and cook for 5-7 minutes, stirring occasionally, until softened.
3. Stir in the diced tomatoes, tomato paste, paprika, chili flakes, vegetable broth, salt, and pepper.
4. Bring the stew to a simmer and cook for 20-25 minutes, until the eggplant is tender and the flavors have melded together.
5. Serve warm, garnished with fresh herbs if desired.

Grilled Asparagus with Lemon and Parmesan

Ingredients:

- **1 lb asparagus**, trimmed
- **2 tbsp olive oil**
- **1/2 tsp garlic powder**
- **Zest of 1 lemon**
- **1/4 cup grated Parmesan cheese**
- **Salt and pepper** to taste

Instructions:

1. Preheat the grill to medium-high heat.
2. Toss the asparagus with olive oil, garlic powder, salt, and pepper.
3. Grill the asparagus for 5-7 minutes, turning occasionally, until tender and slightly charred.
4. Remove from the grill and sprinkle with lemon zest and Parmesan cheese.
5. Serve warm as a zesty, flavorful side dish.

Roasted Pumpkin with Sage and Garlic

Ingredients:

- **1 small pumpkin**, peeled, seeded, and cut into cubes
- **2 tbsp olive oil**
- **4-5 fresh sage leaves**, chopped
- **3 cloves garlic**, minced
- **Salt and pepper** to taste

Instructions:

1. Preheat the oven to 375°F (190°C). Line a baking sheet with parchment paper.
2. Toss the pumpkin cubes with olive oil, chopped sage, garlic, salt, and pepper.
3. Spread the cubes evenly on the baking sheet and roast for 25-30 minutes, until tender and caramelized.
4. Serve warm as a sweet and savory side dish.

Stuffed Acorn Squash with Quinoa

Ingredients:

- **2 acorn squash**, halved and seeds removed
- **1 cup quinoa**, cooked
- **1/2 cup dried cranberries**
- **1/4 cup toasted pumpkin seeds**
- **1 tsp ground cinnamon**
- **1 tbsp olive oil**
- **Salt and pepper** to taste

Instructions:

1. Preheat the oven to 375°F (190°C). Place the squash halves on a baking sheet, cut side up.
2. Drizzle with olive oil, season with salt and pepper, and roast for 35-40 minutes, until tender.
3. While the squash roasts, cook the quinoa according to package instructions.
4. In a bowl, combine the cooked quinoa, cranberries, pumpkin seeds, and cinnamon.
5. Once the squash is cooked, stuff each half with the quinoa mixture.
6. Serve warm as a hearty and nutritious fall dish.

www.ingramcontent.com/pod-product-compliance
Lightning Source LLC
LaVergne TN
LVHW081503060526
838201LV00056BA/2903